The Author

Suzan St Maur is an international business writer and author of 15 published non-fiction business and consumer books.

A keen horsewoman, she lives in a small village in Bedfordshire with her teenage son and numerous other animals.

For more information about Suzan and her other publications see Suzan's website: www.suzanstmaur.com See also her humourous weblog for cancer warriors: www. CancerComicStrip.blogspot.com

The Illustrator

Roger Penwill is a freelance cartoonist and cartoon illustrator. An ex-architect, he is married with two grown up children and lives and works in his home near Ludlow.

He is the originator of the Shrewsbury Cartoon Festival and is the international Vice-President of the Federation of Cartoonists Organisations.

First published by Merlin Unwin Books, 2006.

Text © Suzan St Maur
Illustrations © Roger Penwill

Published by:
Merlin Unwin Books
Palmers House, 7 Corve Street
Ludlow, Shropshire SY8 1DB (U.K.)
www.merlinunwin.co.uk

British Library Cataloguing-in-Publication Data:
A catalogue record for this book is available from the British Library.
The author asserts her right to be identified with this work.

ISBN 1 873674 92 9
ISBN 978 1 873674 92 5

Designed and typeset by Merlin Unwin Books, Ludlow.
Printed in Great Britain by TJ International, Padstow.

The
COUNTRY-LOVER'S
JOKE
Book

Suzan St Maur

Illustrated by Roger Penwill

Merlin Unwin Books

DEDICATION

For Cancer Warriors everywhere
– I know just how therapeutic laughter can be.

Suze

Seeing the light

On a small farm in a remote Welsh valley, Mrs Jones went into labour in the middle of the night, and the doctor was called out to assist in the delivery.

To keep the nervous father-to-be busy, the doctor handed him a lantern and said, 'Here, you hold this high so I can see what I'm doing.' Soon, a baby boy was brought into the world.

'Now, Mr Jones!' said the doctor. 'Keep that lantern steady, boy... I think there's another one to come.' Sure enough, within minutes he had delivered another little baby.

'No, no, don't be in a hurry to be putting down that lantern, Mr Jones... It seems there's yet another one besides!' cried the doctor.

The new father scratched his head in bewilderment, and then asked the doctor, 'Do you think it's the light that's attracting them?'

Hobbled ahoy

Two men were approaching each other across the market square and each noticed that the other was limping badly.

As they drew level with one another, the first man said, 'What happened to you?'

'Falkland Islands, 1981. You?'

'Cowpat, three minutes ago.'

Pet ceremony

An elderly farmer lived alone in the Irish countryside with a mongrel dog he loved dearly. At the grand old age of 16, the dog finally died and the farmer went to see the parish priest.

'Father, my beloved dog has passed away,' said the farmer. 'Would you say a mass for him?'

The priest replied, 'No, I'm sorry, we cannot hold services for animals in our church. But there's one of those new denominations in the town. There's no telling what they believe, but maybe they'll do something for your dog.'

The farmer said, 'I'll go to see them straight away. Tell me, do you think £20,000 is a large enough donation to them for the service?'

'Ah,' the priest said, 'Now why didn't you tell me the dog was a Roman Catholic?'

Ring of truth

A farmer was at the pub one day having a pint when he noticed an old friend. But what really caught his attention was that this friend was wearing an earring. The farmer knew his old friend to be a fairly conservative fellow, and was intrigued by his sudden change in image. The farmer walked up to him and said, 'I didn't know you were into earrings.'

'Don't make such a fuss, it's only an earring,' the fellow replied sheepishly.

The farmer drank his beer in silence for a few minutes, but then his curiosity got the better of him and he asked, 'So, how long have you been wearing one?'

'Ever since my wife found it in my tractor cab,' the man replied.

Gossips anonymous

Mabel was the typical village gossip and self-appointed guardian of village morals. She was known for sticking her nose into other people's business.

Most local folk thought she was an interfering nuisance, but feared her so much that they were careful how they treated her. However, Brian – a strong-minded local farmer – wasn't having any of Mabel's nonsense.

After having spotted Brian's tractor parked outside the village pub all afternoon, Mabel firmly declared Brian to be an alcoholic.

On hearing this, Brian waited until dark, parked his tractor outside Mabel's house – and left it there all night.

Cure or kill

Students from the college of veterinary medicine had been out on the town, celebrating the end of term for several evenings in a row, and complaints from local residents had filtered back to the powers-that-be. As a result, one of the senior lecturers decided to admonish the students and warn them of the perils of drinking alcohol.

At the beginning of his next lecture, he placed one worm in a glass of water, and another in a glass of whisky. After he had delivered his stern warnings about the effects of alcohol on the human body, he pointed to the two glasses on the lectern. The worm in water was still wriggling about, but the worm in the whisky was lying dead at the bottom of the glass.

'Now,' growled the lecturer to his students, 'what conclusion do you draw from this demonstration?'

A voice at the back of the room piped up, 'If your dog has worms, make him drink whisky.'

Service charges

A young farmer's daughter answered the door, and there stood an elderly neighbour. 'My father isn't at home,' she said, 'but I can help you. If you want a bull to service your cow, my father charges one hundred pounds for his best bull.'

"That's not what I want,' the neighbour said.

'We have a young bull that is just starting out. My father charges fifty pounds for him.'

'That's not what I want, either.'

'We have an old bull out in the paddock,' the girl continued. 'He can still do the job, and my father only charges ten pounds for him.'

'That's not what I want,' the neighbour said. 'I came here to see your father about your brother Archie. Archie got my daughter pregnant.'

'Oh,' the girl replied. 'You'll have to see my father about that. I don't know what he charges for Archie.'

Solo soul

A tourist driving through County Fermanagh passed a young man walking along wearing only one shoe.

The driver stopped his car and asked the boy, 'I say young man, have you lost a shoe?'

'No, sure,' the boy replied. 'I've just found one.'

If I could read your mind

At a village fete, a young man saw a small tent, with a sign above saying, 'For £5, I'll teach you to be a mind-reader! - Apply within.'

The young man thought he'd give it a go, and went inside. Behind a small table sat an old man, who looked up and said, 'Ah, you must be here for the mind-reading lesson.'

'Er, yes,' the young man said.

So the old man went out the back of the tent and came back with a hose. 'Here, hold this hose,' he said.

'Why?' asked the young man.

'It's part of the lesson,' replied the old man, 'Now, look in the end and tell me what you see.'

Puzzled, the young man looked into the end of the hose. 'I don't see anything,' he said.

Just then the old man turned on the tap, and the hose shot water into the young man's face.

'I just knew you'd do something like that!' the young man shouted.

'Excellent - you're a mind reader!' the old man replied. 'That'll be £5 please.'

Like father, like son

The Head of Admissions of Harper Adams Agricultural College was interviewing a prospective student, 'Why have you chosen this career?' he asked.

'I dream of making ten million pounds in farming, like my father,' the student replied.

'Your father made ten million pounds in farming?' echoed the Head, much impressed.

'No,' replied the applicant. 'But he always dreamed of it.'

Eager eagles

A Golden Eagle came swooping in from the night sky, covered from head to tail in fresh blood, and settled down exhausted on the rock edge to get some sleep.

Pretty soon all the other eagles smelled the blood and began pestering at him to say where he made such a major kill. He told them to shut up and let him go to sleep but they persisted, until finally he gave in.

'OK!' he said with exasperation, 'Follow me,' and he glided off the mountain ledge with all the other eagles following closely behind him. Down through the glens they went, past the rushing waterfalls and into the deep forest.

Finally he slowed down and all the other eagles excitedly gathered around him.

'Do you see that tree over there?' he asked.

'Yes, yes, yes!' the eagles all screamed in a frenzy.

'Good,' he said, 'Because I DIDN'T!'

A pot for two

A young man visited his sister who was married to a farmer in Cumbria. As accommodation was limited, he was obliged to share a bed with his young nephew.

In the bedroom, he saw his little nephew kneeling at the side of the bed with his head bowed.

Impressed by the child's religious upbringing, he decided to match this good example and kneeled at the other side of the bed, also with his head bowed.

The boy looked up and said, 'What are you doing?'

'Well, the same as you're doing,' replied the Uncle.

'Mum's going to be right browned off,' said the boy. 'The pot's on this side.'

Learning curve

A townie moved from London to the Cotswolds and decided to take up farming. He went off to the supplier near his new smallholding and said to the assistant, '100 baby chickens, please.' The assistant duly produced 100 chicks.

A week later the man was back, and said to the same assistant, 'I'd like 200 baby chickens, please.' The assistant complied.

A further week later, the man was back again. This time he asked, 'Please may I have 500 baby chickens?'

'Goodness!' the assistant replied. 'You must be doing well!'

'Well, not really,' said the man, looking perplexed. 'I can't quite work it out yet, but I reckon I'm either planting them too deep or too far apart...'

Trigger happy

A couple of farm lads in Cornwall were out in the fields shooting rabbits. One of them suddenly fell to the ground, stopped breathing, and his eyes rolled to the back of his head.

His friend pulled out his mobile phone, called the emergency services, and gasped to the operator, 'My friend is dead! What should I do?'

The operator, in a professional, soothing voice said, 'Keep calm and follow this procedure, step-by-step. First, let's make sure he's dead.'

There was a silence, then a shot rang out.

'OK,' said the lad returning to his phone. 'Now what?'

Well-intentioned...

A beef farmer wishing to increase the size of his herd asked his young son to take their cow over to the bull at the far side of the village. As the small boy was leading the cow down the lanes, they met the local priest.

'Where are you going?' asked the vicar, concerned that such a little lad was in charge of such a large animal.

'I'm taking the cow to the bull, Vicar,' said the boy.

'Couldn't your father help? Or perhaps I could do it?'

'No, sorry, Vicar. It has to be the bull.'

More goat Vicar?

A young couple invited their elderly vicar for Sunday lunch.

While the hosts were in the kitchen preparing the meal, the vicar asked their son what they were having to eat.

'Goat,' the little boy said.

'Goat?' asked the startled vicar, 'Are you sure about that?'

'Yep,' said the boy. 'I heard Dad say to Mum, 'Might as well have the old goat for lunch today as any other day.'

Bull market

A man took his wife to a county show in northern England, and they wandered past the pens that housed the prize bulls. The sign on the first bull's pen stated: 'This bull mated 50 times last year.'

The wife turned to her husband and said, 'He mated 50 times in a year: isn't that nice!'

They proceeded to the next bull and his sign stated: 'This bull mated 65 times last year.' The wife turned to her husband and said, 'This one mated 65 times last year. That's over five times a month! You could learn from this one!'

They carried on until they reached the last bull, and his sign said: 'This bull mated 365 times last year.' The wife's mouth dropped open and she said, 'Goodness me! He mated 365 times last year. That's ONCE A DAY!! You could really learn from this one.'

The man, by now fed up, turned to his wife and said, 'Listen, love, why don't you go to the show secretary's tent and enquire if that was 365 times with the same cow?'

Not a bitter pill

A couple of old farmers were discussing their livestock one market day. One said, 'I don't know what's wrong with my bull but he just hasn't been able to manage it for nearly a month now.'

'Ah, not to worry,' said the other farmer, 'that new vet in Abbots Bradwell gave us some amazing pills for that very problem. I only had to give my old fellow one pill and he was back to his old self again within minutes. Serviced all the cows and even had plenty to spare for artificial insemination.'

'Great,' said the first farmer. 'What are those pills called? I must get some for my bull.'

'Can't remember the name offhand,' replied the second farmer, 'but they're round, about the size of a coat button, pale blue in colour and they taste of vanilla.'

More powerful pills

Concerned about his failing manhood, a farmer went to the local doctor for help. The doctor gave him a small container of pills and told him to take no more than one a day.

Back home, the farmer thought he'd try out the medication on his prize bull first. The bull swallowed the pill, jumped out of his paddock, rammed an entire side wall of the barn until it was no more than rubble and ran off down the road, snorting wildly. 'Those pills are too strong for me,' the farmer thought, and poured the rest into his well.

Next time he was at the surgery, the farmer told the doctor how he had disposed of the unwanted medication.

'Good Lord!' exclaimed the doctor. 'You haven't drunk any of the well water, have you?'

'No,' said the farmer. 'We can't get the pump handle down.'

Which hat to wear

In a small crofting community in the Scottish Highlands, the local policeman also fulfilled the role of the village vet, having qualified in that discipline before joining the police. Late one night his phone rang, and his wife answered.

A distraught voice cried, 'I need to speak to your husband – urgently!'

'Do you need him as the policeman or as the vet?' asked his wife.

'Both,' came the response. 'We can't get the dog's mouth open, and there's a burglar in it.'

Identity crisis

A Somerset farmer couldn't tell his two cows apart, so he tried cutting one cow's tail a little shorter than the other's. This worked for a while, until the cow's tail hairs grew again. Then the farmer tried trimming the horns of one cow, which also worked until they grew out. Finally, the farmer found a long-term solution – to measure the cows. And when he did, he discovered that the grey one was at least four inches taller than the brown one.

No bailing out

A vicar walks down a country lane and sees a young farmer struggling to load straw bales back onto a trailer they had fallen from.

'You look hot, my son,' said the vicar, 'Why don't you rest a moment, and then I will help you?'

'No thank you,' said the young man, 'My Dad wouldn't like it.'

'Don't be silly,' the vicar said. 'Everyone is entitled to a break.'

Again the young man protested that his father would be upset. Losing his patience, the vicar said, 'Your father must be a real tyrant. Tell me where I can find him and I'll give him a piece of my mind!'

'Well, that's just it,' replied the young farmer. 'He's under the bales.'

Cow on wheels

A salesman was trying to talk a farmer into buying a bicycle, but was meeting with considerable sales resistance.

'I'd rather spend my money on a cow,' said the farmer.

'Ah,' replied the salesman, 'but think how stupid you'd look riding a cow.'

'Maybe,' replied the farmer, 'but not as stupid as I'd look trying to milk a bicycle.'

Back to basics

The Third Thursday Club, an organization of wealthy Birmingham women, decided to have an outing to a dairy farm. Most of them had lived in the city all their lives, and had never seen such a thing.

The day came, and the ladies filed into the rented coach which whisked them off to their destination. On the way, they watched out the windows as the city squalor turned into lovely, unpolluted countryside.

On arrival, they were greeted by the farmer who invited them to look him up should they have any questions. Audrey, after looking about and being amazed by what she saw, stepped into a building and viewed something she thought was quite remarkable. She saw the farmer walk by and hailed him – he sauntered in.

'I was just wondering,' she said, 'Why this cow doesn't have any horns?'

The farmer cocked his head for a moment, then began in a patient tone: 'Well, cattle can do a lot of damage with horns. Sometimes we keep 'em trimmed down with a hacksaw. Other times we can sort out the young ones by puttin' a couple of drops of acid where their horns would grow, and that stops 'em cold. And then again, there are some breeds of cattle that never grow horns. But the reason this cow don't have no horns is 'cause it's a horse.'

Politics of a dairy herd

TRADITIONAL CAPITALISM:
You have two cows.
You sell one and buy a bull.
Your herd expands, and the economy grows.
You sell the herd and retire on the proceeds.

A FRENCH CORPORATION:
You have two cows.
You go on strike because you want three cows.

A GERMAN CORPORATION:
You have two cows.
You re-engineer them so they live for 100 years, eat once a month, and milk themselves.

A BRITISH CORPORATION:
You have two cows.
Both are mad.

AN ITALIAN CORPORATION:
You have two cows, but you don't know where they are.
You break for lunch.

A CHINESE CORPORATION:
You have two cows.
You have 300 people milking each one.
You claim full employment, high dairy herd productivity, and imprison the journalist who reported the numbers.

A JAPANESE CORPORATION:

You have two cows.

You redesign them so they are one-tenth the size of an ordinary cow and produce twenty times the milk.

You then create clever cow cartoon images called Cowkemon and market them worldwide.

A RUSSIAN CORPORATION:

You have two cows.

You count them and discover you have five cows.

You count them again and discover you have 42 cows.

You count them again and discover you have 12 cows.

You stop counting cows and open another bottle of vodka.

A SWISS CORPORATION:

You have 5,000 cows, none of which belongs to you.

You charge their owners huge amounts for storing them.

A HINDU CORPORATION:

You have two cows.

You worship them.

AN AMERICAN CORPORATION:

You have two cows.

You sell one, and make the other one produce the milk of four cows.

You are surprised when your remaining cow drops dead.

VENTURE CAPITALISM:

You have two cows.

You sell three of them to your publicly listed company, using letters of credit opened by your brother-in-law at the bank, then execute a debt/equity swap with an associated general offer so that you get all four cows back, with a tax exemption for five cows.

The milk rights of the six cows are transferred via an intermediary to a Cayman Island company secretly owned by the majority shareholder who sells the rights to all seven cows back to your listed company.

The annual report says the company owns eight cows, with an option on one more.

You sell one cow to buy a new president of the United States, leaving you with nine cows.

No balance sheet provided with the flotation.

The public buys your bull.

Once a professional

A vet had been invited to an important Chamber of Commerce dinner in the town and was held up during the pre-dinner drinks by a woman who buttonholed him, asking endless questions about her goats and their various health problems. When the vet eventually reached the dinner table, he found he was sitting next to a solicitor, to whom he complained about the woman.

'Do you think I should send her a bill?' asked the vet.

'Of course you should,' smiled the solicitor. 'You were delivering veterinary consultation.'

The next day when the vet opened his post at the surgery, he found a letter from the solicitor accompanied by an invoice 'To legal consultation, £50.'

Hell hath no fury...

Three Hell's Angel motorbikers went into a small transport café on the edge of a Worcestershire village. They went up to an old farmer at the table where he was having his breakfast.

The first biker took out his cigarette and dropped it into the farmer's tea.

The farmer didn't say a word and resumed eating his breakfast.

The second biker tipped over the farmer's glass of orange juice.

Still no reaction.

The third biker picked up the old farmer's fried breakfast and threw it on the floor.

The farmer got up without saying a word, paid his bill and left the café.

'He wasn't much of a man was he?' stated the leader of the pack.

'No,' said the waitress, looking out of the window. 'And he's not much of a driver either. He just backed a huge tractor and trailer full of hay bales over three Harley Davidson motorbikes.'

Keep it in the family

A millionaire potato-grower in Norfolk welcomed his new son-in-law into the family.

'Jeremy,' he said, 'you have married my favourite daughter and to show how much I value you as her husband, I would like to welcome you as a 50-50 partner in the potato business. All you have to do is to come in every day and learn about potatoes and sowing.'

'But I can't stand farming,' said the son-in-law. 'I hate early mornings and I can't drive a tractor.'

'Very well,' said the father-in-law. 'You can work in the office and manage the administration.'

'I hate office work,' replied the son-in-law. 'I can't stand being stuck behind a desk all day.'

'Hang on a minute,' said the father-in-law. 'I just made you a half-owner of a profitable potato empire, but you don't like the outdoor life and won't work in the office. What am I going to do with you?'

'That's easy,' said the son-in-law. 'Buy me out.'

A burst of speed

Shortly before the start of the main point-to-point race of the day, the chief steward saw one of the owners slip something into his horse's mouth. The chief steward stormed across to the man and asked if he was trying to drug the horse.

'Of course not,' said the owner. 'I was just giving him a lump of sugar. Here – let me prove to you that's there nothing in it. I've just given one lump to the horse. I'll eat the second and you eat the third.'

Suspicious but willing to trust, the chief steward took the proffered sugar lump and ate it. The owner ate his, and the steward walked off. Just then the horse's jockey came up for his last-minute briefing from the horse's owner.

'OK, Johnnie,' said the owner, 'Hold him back for the first three furlongs and then let him go flat out. I promise you, nothing will get past him, other than perhaps me or the chief steward.'

No accounting for taste

A bullock strolled into the local pub at lunchtime and ordered sausage and chips with mustard, ketchup and vinegar. As the bullock tucked in, the landlady stared at him.

'I expect you find it strange that a bullock should come into your pub and order a meal like this,' said the bullock.

'Not at all,' said the landlady. 'I always have mustard, ketchup and vinegar with my sausage and chips too.'

Futures and options

A little boy was looking at the red ripe tomatoes growing in the farmer's garden. 'I'll give you both my pennies for that tomato,' said the boy, pointing to a beautiful, large, ripe one hanging on the vine.

'No,' said the farmer, 'I get ten pence for a tomato like that one.'

The small boy pointed to a smaller green one, 'Will you take two pence for that one?'

'Yes,' agreed the farmer, 'I'll give you that one for two pence.'

'OK,' said the lad, finalising the deal as he put the coins in the farmer's hand, 'I'll be back for it in about a week.'

Straight from the vet's notes...

1. On the 2nd day the hock was better and on the 3rd day it disappeared completely.

2. Clinic discharge status: alive but without permission of owner.

3. Past veterinary history has been remarkably insignificant with only a 50 kilogram weight gain in the past three days.

4. Between you and me, we ought to be able to get this cow in calf.

5. Since we can't get her in calf with AI, I thought you might like to work her up.

6. He is numb from his hoofs down.

7. The nostrils were moist and dry.

8. Occasional, constant, infrequent coughing.

9. Sheep was alert and unresponsive.

10. Rectal examination revealed a normal size throat.

11. The lab test indicated abnormal lover function.

12. Eyes: somewhat dull but present.

13. Filly was seen in consultation by Mr. Blank, who felt we should sit on the tendon and I agree.

14. Ewe has had one healthy lamb, but no other abnormalities.

Long term support

The owner of a llama farm in Buckinghamshire was notoriously slow in settling his bills. In the end the local veterinary practice got so fed up with him that the senior partner wrote to him personally, saying 'Considering that we've done more for you than your own mother, we would be grateful if you would settle your account immediately.' The llama-breeder phoned a couple of days later and said, 'What do you mean, you did more for me than my mother did?'

'Well,' replied the senior vet, 'According to our records we've been carrying you for the last 15 months.'

Vettus interruptus

Long after midnight, an elderly farmer's wife was awakened by a noise outside her bedroom window. She went to the window and across the farmyard she could just make out a dog and a bitch that were mating rather noisily a few yards away.

Furious, she rushed to the telephone and rang up the vet, demanding that he do something about it.

'Mrs Jones,' said the vet down the phone, 'it's way past midnight and you have just got me out of bed. Might I suggest you tell those dogs that they're wanted on the telephone?'

'Why?' she responded. 'Will that stop them?'

'Well, put it this way, Mrs Jones,' said the vet. 'It has certainly had that effect on me.'

Survival of the fittest

Two ramblers, both in their 60s, were walking through the dales.

A huge black bull suddenly appeared on the brow of a hill about 50 feet in front of them. The bull eyed them up and began to paw the ground.

Joe dropped his backpack, dug out a pair of running shoes, and frantically began to put them on.

His friend Jack yelled, 'What are you doing? Trainers won't help you outrun that bull.'

'I don't need to outrun the bull,' Joe replied. 'I just need to outrun you.'

Going up in the world

A crofter family from the Isle of Lewis visited the city for the first time and decided to visit a super-multiplex shopping centre. The father and son were strolling around while the wife shopped. They were amazed by almost everything they saw, but especially by two shiny, silver doors that could slide apart and then slide back together again.

The boy asked, 'Dad, what's that?'

The father (never having seen a lift before) said, 'Son, I nivver saw anything like that in ma entire life, I dinna ken what it is.'

While the boy and his father were watching with amazement, a fat old lady went up to the moving doors and pressed a button. The doors opened and the lady entered into a small room. The doors closed and the two bumpkins watched the numbers above the doors light up: 1, 2, 3, 4. They watched until it reached the last number and then the numbers began to light in the reverse order. Then the doors opened again and out stepped a gorgeous, voluptuous young blonde woman.

The father, his eyes riveted on the young woman, said quietly to his son, 'Hamish, run quick and fetch yer mother...'

Green horn

After much urging by his wife, Fred applied for work on a local farm. The farm manager agreed to give him a try and

told him to milk a cow, equipping him with a stool and a bucket.

An hour later Fred returned dirty and sweaty, the bucket in one hand and a broken stool in the other.

'Getting the milk out was easy,' he explained. 'The worst part was getting the cow to sit on the stool.'

Mirror, mirror

After living in the remote fens of East Anglia all his life, an old potato farmer decided it was time to visit the big city. In one of the shops he picked up a mirror and looked in it. Not knowing what it was, he remarked, 'How about that! Here's a picture of my daddy.'

He bought the 'picture,' but on the way home he remembered his wife, Daphne, didn't like his father. So he hung the picture in the barn, and every morning before leaving for the fields, he would go there and look at it.

Daphne began to get suspicious of these many trips to the barn. One day after her husband left, she searched the barn and found the mirror. As she looked into the glass, she fumed, 'So that's the ugly witch he's runnin' around with!'

Chicken stew

Two yokels were walking toward each other across a field. One was carrying a sack. When they met, one said, 'Hey Bert, what have you got in that bag?'

'Some chickens.'

'If I guess how many are in there, can I have one?'

'Listen …. if you guess right, I'll give you both of 'em!'

'Arrrr …. ummmmm …. five?'

Terrible tools

One night, a young woman drove to the local police station and ran in, sporting a huge black eye. When interrogated she stated that she had heard a noise in her front garden and had gone to investigate. The next thing she knew, she had been hit in the face and was knocked out, unconscious.

An officer in a police car was duly despatched to her remote cottage to investigate. He returned half an hour later with a black eye.

'Have you been attacked by the same person?' the desk sergeant asked.

'No,' replied the PC. 'I stepped on the same rake.'

Digging up trouble

During the troubles in Northern Ireland, an old man, living alone near the Border, wanted to dig the potato patch on his allotment. But, being rather frail, he found it too difficult. His only son, who usually helped him, was in prison for terrorist offences. The old man wrote his son a letter and mentioned the problems he faced with his potato patch. Soon after he received this reply, 'For HEAVEN'S SAKE, Da, don't dig up your potato patch. That's where I buried THE GUNS!'

At 4 o'clock the next morning, a dozen British soldiers arrived and dug up the entire potato patch and, having found no guns, left without a word. Confused, the old man wrote to his son in prison telling him what had happened, and asking what he should do next. His son replied, 'Now it should be easy for you to plant your potatoes, Da. That was the best I could do, sure!'

Strife in Fife

A London-based QC went duck shooting in deepest Fife, where the Kings of Scotland hunted in days of old. The barrister shot a perfect specimen, but it fell into a field on the other side of a fence. As the barrister climbed over the fence to retrieve it, an elderly farmer drove up on his tractor and asked him what he was doing. The barrister responded, 'I shot a duck and it fell in your field, and now I'm going into your field to retrieve it.'

The old farmer replied, 'This is private property, and yer no comin' ower here.'

The indignant barrister said, 'I am one of the best QCs in the UK and if you don't allow me access to that duck, I'll sue you and take everything you own.'

The old farmer smiled and said, 'Apparently, you dinna ken how we do things in Scotland. We settle small disagreements like this wi' the Fife Three Kick Rule.'

The barrister asked, 'And what is the Fife Three Kick Rule?'

The farmer replied, 'Weel, first I kick you three times and then you kick me three times, and so on, back and forth, until someone gives up.' The barrister eyed up the old farmer and decided that he could easily take him on. So he agreed to abide by the local custom.

The old farmer slowly climbed down from the tractor and walked up to the barrister. His first kick planted the toe of his heavy work boot into the barrister's groin and felled him to his knees. His second kick threw him backwards. The barrister was flat in the mud when the farmer's third kick nearly caused him to give up.

The barrister summoned every bit of his will, managed to get to his feet and said, 'Okay, you old so-and-so. Now it's my turn.'

The old farmer smiled at him and said, 'Nae, I gie up. Ye can hae the duck.'

Named and shamed

A farmer was sued by a village post-mistress for defamation of character. She alleged that he had called her a pig. The farmer was found guilty and fined.

Just before they left the Courtroom the farmer asked the judge, 'Your Honour, does this mean that I can't call Mrs Johnson a pig?' The judge nodded and affirmed that this was the case.

'Does this also mean that I can't use the words, 'Mrs Johnson', to name a pig?' the farmer continued. The judge considered for a moment, then replied that to his knowledge there was no law against using the words 'Mrs Johnson' to name a pig.

The farmer looked directly at his accuser, who was still smirking triumphantly, and with a nod of his head said, 'Goodbye, Mrs. Johnson.'

Ham-fisted

Two farmers in Leicestershire had a quarrel over a piece of land and eventually the whole thing went to the County Court. Stan, one of the farmers, was a wily old fellow and everyone around knew that he had been the transgressor, but his solicitor was amazed when he won the case.

When he asked Stan why he thought the judge had found in his favour, Stan said, 'Simple. I sent the judge a smoked ham.' The solicitor was horrified, of course, and said he could have been done for attempted bribery as well as losing the case.

Stan just smiled and said, 'Ah, yes, but I sent it in the other farmer's name.'

Male chauvinist pig

In a Yorkshire village, farmers of the community had got together to discuss some important issues. About half way through the meeting, a wife of one of the farmers stood up and said her piece.

One of the old farmers heckled her: 'What does she know about anything? I would like to ask her if she knows how many toes a pig has?'

Quick as a flash, the woman replied, 'Take off your boots sir, and count them yourself.'

Fair exchange

A London couple were holidaying in Scotland and had been invited to shoot grouse on a private estate belonging to some wealthy, titled friends. The shoot progressed as anticipated although the grouse were not plentiful. Suddenly the London man thought he had struck lucky and blasted into some gorse near the other members of the party.

'I say, Cartwright,' shouted his Lordship 'you almost hit my wife!'

'Good Lord, awfully sorry,' cried the Londoner, horrified. 'Here, take a shot at mine. She's over there.'

A likely story

The fishing season hadn't yet opened and a fisherman, who didn't have a licence, was casting for trout when a stranger approached and asked:

'Any luck?'

'Any luck? This is a wonderful spot. I took 10 trout out of this stream yesterday,' he boasted.

'Really? By the way, do you know who I am?' asked the stranger.

'No.'

'Well, meet the new river-keeper.'

'Oh,' gulped the fisherman. 'Well, do you know who I am?'

'No.'

'Meet the biggest liar in Ayrshire.'

Bring him down to size

A farmer from Texas was visiting England and got chatting with a local farmer in the village pub. They were discussing the size of farms in America versus those in the UK.

'You know, I get in my truck in the morning, and I could drive it from sunrise to sunset and still not get around the whole of my property,' bragged the Texan.

'I do understand,' replied the British farmer. 'I had a truck like that a few years ago.'

Mechanic in sheep's clothing

In the middle of nowhere, a man's car broke down. He got out and was peering under the bonnet to see what was wrong, when a ewe trotted up to the nearby fence and looked over at the car. 'Probably the cam belt gone,' said the ewe.

The man was so shocked by this that he ran off down the road until he bumped into a farmer. He told the farmer what had just happened.

'Was it a big fluffy sheep with longish ears?' asked the farmer.

'Yes, I think so,' said the man.

'Oh, don't listen to her,' said the farmer. 'She doesn't know a thing about cars.'

You're where?

Some years ago a man was towing his boat back to Hampshire after a sea fishing trip in Cornwall when his car broke down on the A30. This was before the days of mobile phones and – it being late at night – there was no-one around, so he decided to use his marine radio to get help. Climbing into his boat, he broadcast his call letters and asked for assistance.

A Coast Guard officer responded, 'Please give your location.'

'I'm on the A30 about five miles north-east of Penzance.'

The officer paused, 'Could you repeat that?'

'A30, five miles north-east of Penzance.'

A longer pause. Then an incredulous voice asked, 'How fast were you going when you hit the beach?'

Proud cockerel

The minister had just finished an excellent chicken dinner at the home of one of his parishioners. Sitting on the verandah after dinner, he saw a cockerel go strutting by. 'That's certainly a proud-looking cockerel you have there,' the minister commented.

'Yes, indeed,' replied the farmer. 'He has reason to be proud; one of his sons just entered the ministry.'

Survival tips for campers

First of all, take this simple test to see if you qualify for solo camping: shine a flashlight into one ear. If the beam shines out the other ear, do not go into the woods alone.

You can start a fire without matches by eating an Indian take-away, then breathing on a pile of dry sticks.

The guitar of the noisy teenager at the next campsite makes excellent kindling.

The glimpsed sighting of a bald eagle has thrilled campers for generations. The sight of a bald man, however, does absolutely nothing for the eagle.

It's entirely possible to spend your whole holiday on a

winding road behind a large caravan.

In an emergency, you can survive in the wilderness by shooting small game with a catapult made from the elastic waistband of your underwear.

In an emergency, a drawstring from a parka hood can be used to strangle a snoring tent-mate.

Stating the obvious

Sherlock Holmes and Dr. Watson went on a camping holiday in Dorset. After a good meal, a bottle of wine and a little violin playing around the campfire, they settled down for the night and went to sleep.

Some hours later, Holmes awoke and nudged his companion. 'Watson, raise your eyes and tell me what you observe.'

Watson replied, 'I observe millions of stars.'

'What does that indicate to you?'

Watson thought for a moment. 'Astronomically, it indicates that there are millions of galaxies and probably billions of planets. Astrologically, I observe that Pluto is in Pisces. Horologically, I estimate that the time is approximately oh four hundred hours. Theologically, I feel that God is all powerful and that we are tiny and insignificant. Meteorologically, I predict that we will enjoy a fine day tomorrow. Why, what does it indicate to you?'

Holmes was speechless for a moment, then spoke. 'Watson, you are an idiot. Some so-and-so has stolen our tent.'

Mule trouble

Two old boys from Somerset bought a new mule, but had trouble getting it into their barn. Every time they would get him to the door, his ears would brush the top of the doorway and he'd start kicking and go berserk. Finally, they decided the best way to solve the problem was to jack up the barn. So, they went out and got a half dozen jacks.

The two men were scrambling from jack to jack to try to get the barn raised when the local pig farmer walked up. 'What be you up to?' he asked.

'We're raisin' the barn, stupid,' said Jethro.

'Whatever makes you want to do that for then?'

''Cause the mule's ears keep touchin' the doorway when we try to put him in this-here barn and he goes berserk, he does,' Old Tom said. 'He kicked Jethro plumb in the head twice already.'

'Well in that case, why doesn't you jus' dig a hole in the doorway? Like that, see, he'll have to step down when he reaches the doorway and his big ol' ears won't touch nothin'.'

'You old fool,' said Jethro. 'It's his ears what are too long, not his legs!'

In loving memory

The Master of Foxhounds and the Whipper-In were leading a small mid-week field, trotting along a lane to the next field. Along the lane came a funeral cortege. The Whipper-

In pulled his horse up and solemnly took off his cap.

'Delighted to see you still observe the old-fashioned courtesies, Curtis,' said the Master, also pulling his horse up as hounds milled around impatiently. 'Not enough good manners around these days.'

The Whipper-In replaced his cap and prepared to move off again. 'Thank you, Sir,' he said. 'But to be fair, we were married for thirty-two years.'

Not amused

A white cockerel was strutting around the henhouse one Easter morning when he came across a nest of eggs dyed every colour of the rainbow.

He took one look at the colourful display, ran outside and thrashed the living daylights out of the resident peacock.

Surprises rule

A farmer had a black cow and a white cow and he wanted them to be mated. He borrowed the neighbouring farmer's bull and turned it out in the paddock with them. He called his young son and asked him to keep watch and let him know when the bull had done his business.

'Yes Dad, yes Dad,' said the little boy eagerly.

After a while the little boy went into the kitchen where his Dad was talking with some feed reps. 'Hey, Dad,' said the boy.

'Yes,' replied his father.

'The bull just bonked the black cow.'

There was a silence in the room. The farmer said 'Excuse us a moment,' and took his son outside. 'Michael, you mustn't use words like that. Not when there's company, or ever. You should say 'The bull surprised the black cow'. Now go out to the paddock and come back and tell me when the bull surprises the white cow.'

The farmer returned to the kitchen. After a while the boy came back and said, 'Hey, Dad!'

'Yes, Michael. Did the bull surprise the white cow?'

'I'll say he did, Dad! He only went and bonked the black cow again!'

Philofishy

A father and son went fishing one day. After an hour out in the boat, the boy started asking his father questions, 'Dad, how does the boat float?' Father thought for a moment, then admitted, 'I don't know, son.'

The boy was silent for a few minutes and then asked, 'Dad, how do fish breathe underwater?'

Once again the father replied, 'Don't know, son.'

A little later, the boy asked, 'Why is the sky blue?'

Again, the father replied. 'Don't know, son.'

Worried he was beginning to annoy his father, he says, 'Dad, do you mind me asking you all of these questions?'

'Of course not, son. If you don't ask questions… you'll never learn anything!'

Crashing bore

A local Hunt had organised a black-tie dinner, and had asked their local MP to make an after-dinner speech. As his speech droned on and on, one huntsman who was considerably the worse for drink, couldn't take it any more and lobbed an empty wine bottle at the MP. Unfortunately, the bottle hit the MFH instead.

'Hit me again,' murmured the MFH as he slumped lower in his chair, 'I can still hear the old so-and-so.'

Pet fish

A man with two buckets of fish was stopped by a water bailiff in the Lake District as he was leaving a lake well known for its fishing. The bailiff asked the man, 'Do you have a licence to catch those fish?'

The man replied, 'No. These are my pet fish.'

'Pet fish?'

'Yes, sir. Every night I take these fish down to the lake and let them swim around for a while. Then I whistle and they jump back into their buckets, and I take 'em home.'

'That's rubbish! Fish can't do that!'

The man looked at the bailiff for a moment, and then said, 'All right, I'll show you how they do it.'

'This I must see!' said the bailiff, by now intrigued. The man tipped the fish into the lake and stood back and waited. After several minutes, the bailiff turned to the man and said, 'Well?'

'Well, what?' the man responded.

'When are you going to call them back?' the water bailiff prompted.

'Call who back?' the man asked.

'The fish.'

'What fish?' the man asked, with a sly grin

Fate worse than death?

Young David had never been on a shark-fishing expedition before, and he was now deeply regretting it. The sea off the Cornish coast was decidedly choppy and he felt terrible.

Who would ever have believed that sea-sickness could make you feel this awful?

With every pitch and roll, David wondered how he was going to survive the remaining two hours of the trip.

One of the crew felt sorry for him and said, 'Don't worry, young man. No-one's ever died of sea-sickness.'

'Oh nooooo!!' David groaned. 'You've just taken away my last ray of hope.'

Going out with a blast

The local squire had ridden to hounds until he was nearly a hundred. He attributed his long life and good health to his rather unusual habit of a daily pinch of gun powder. When he finally died, he left seven children, 20 grand-children and a 40-foot crater at the crematorium.

Dead woman walking

A professional eventer at Badminton bumped into her childhood riding instructor who was by now an old man. 'How lovely to see you after all these years,' said the old instructor. 'I remember, you're Miss Simpson.'

'That's right,' said his former pupil. 'How clever of you to recognise me after all this time!'

'Now tell me,' continued the old instructor, 'was it you or your sister who was killed in that dreadful riding accident?'

Chicken-hearted

The farmer's son was coming home from the market with the crate of hens his father had entrusted to him, when all of a sudden the box fell and split apart.

On hands and knees he managed to put the crate back together, but in the meantime the hens had scrambled off in all directions. The poor boy ran for miles around the surrounding countryside rounding up all the escaped birds and returned them to the repaired crate. Hoping he had found them all, the boy nervously went back to his farm, expecting the worst.

'Dad, the hens got away,' the boy owned up morosely, 'but I managed to find all fourteen of them.'

'Well, you did a good job there, m' lad,' the farmer smiled. 'You left the market with eight.'

Raring to go

Now in his eighties and retired, the Master of Fox Hounds ran into his old Whipper-In at the Hunt Ball. 'Good to see you again, Spedding,' said the old Master. 'How are things with you?'

'Not so good, Sir, if I'm honest,' replied the Whipper-In. 'In fact I haven't had a decent day's hunting since 1959.'

The Master looked at his watch. 'Well, you're not doing too badly,' he said. 'It's only 20:30 now.'

Diversionary course

'This is the worst cross-country course I've ever ridden in my life,' shouted an irate and muddy competitor to a small group of spectators as she and her horse made a third attempt at some ramshackle hurdles.

'You're half a mile from the course,' one shouted back. 'This is our farmyard.'

Out-laws

A young couple were driving along a country lane on their way home from a weekend with friends in a country cottage. A tense silence prevailed. An earlier conversation had led to an argument, and neither of them was prepared to back down.

As they drove past some brown fields full of snuffling pigs and piglets, the man looked across to his partner and sarcastically sneered, 'I expect they're relations of yours?'

'Funny you should say that, yes they are,' she smiled sweetly. 'I married into the family.'

Wee confusion

One frosty winter's morning a woman was out riding on her large, very fat gelding. When he obstinately refused to move over to the side of the road to make way for a car, she tapped him on the quarters with her whip. As the car drove past a very self-righteous passenger stuck his head out of the window and shouted, 'It's disgusting! Beating that poor mare when she is so obviously pregnant!'

Horse and rider had stopped by this time, and as the car pulled up a few feet away, the gelding decided to use the opportunity to urinate. The local blacksmith, who knew the equine pair, and who had heard the man shout indignantly, strode up to the car window and said, 'Shockin', int' it? Now her waters have broken and there's a leg sticking out.'

Silly buggy

A city man retired and moved to the country. Every morning he put on his tweeds and flat cap and made every effort to become a country gentleman.

One day an old friend from the city came to visit him. As he was showing him around the farm they came to the gentleman's pride and joy ..... a fine-looking horse.

'Yes,' said the gentleman, 'I go for a carriage ride almost every morning. Shall I harness her up and we'll go for a drive?'

'Sounds good,' answered the friend.

The gentleman started to harness the horse, but it wouldn't open its mouth to accept the bit. It was obvious that the former townie had no idea how to tack up a horse, and after the tenth attempt to get the poor creature to open its mouth, his guest said, 'Why don't you just wait until it yawns?'

Impossible dreams

Walking her dog across the fields one day a farmer's wife spotted a Genie's lamp. She picked up the lamp and rubbed it, and lo-and-behold! a Genie appeared. The amazed woman asked if she could have her three wishes.

The Genie said, 'No: due to government cutbacks, a decline in the rural economy, the high value of the pound against the euro and fierce global competition, I can only grant you one wish. So... what'll it be?'

The woman didn't hesitate. She pulled out a document from her jacket pocket and said, 'I want peace in Palestine, Iraq and Afghanistan. See this map? I want these countries to stop fighting.'

The Genie looked at the map and exclaimed, 'You must be joking! These countries have been fighting for decades. I'm good, but not THAT good! Make another wish.'

The woman thought for a minute and then said, 'Well, I've never been able to find a farrier who wasn't late. The hours I spend every year waiting for the farrier to come and do my horse, when I could be putting my time to far better use ..... Yes, that's what I wish for. A good farrier who is always on time.'

The Genie let out a long sigh and said, 'OK, let's have another look at that map.'

Wind direction

A young pupil was very proud that one of the country's most famous carriage driving champions was coming to her yard to give her a private lesson. She had stayed up all the previous night cleaning the harness, the Governess cart and pony. Finally the moment came when they set off in the cart with everything looking fantastic. They were going along splendidly when suddenly the pony rather noisily broke wind.

'Oh gosh, I am sorry about that,' said the young pupil.

'No problem,' smiled the famous champion. 'If you hadn't said anything, I would have thought it was the pony.'

Reverse option

A stockbroker from Chelsea decided to go on a pony-trekking holiday in the West Country, and set off full of confidence, despite the fact that he had never ridden before and knew nothing about horses. After a basic lecture on riding on the first day, the next morning he was cheerfully tacking up his pony when the Head Girl stopped and said, 'You do realise, don't you, that you're putting the saddle on back to front?'

'That's what you think,' replied the cheeky chap. 'You don't know which way I'm going to go!'

Advice to a cowboy

1. Don't squat with your spurs on.

2. Don't interfere with something that ain't bothering you none.

3. If you find yourself in a hole, stop digging.

4. Always drink upstream from the herd.

5. Telling a man to 'git' and making him do it are two entirely different propositions.

6. When you give a personal lesson in meanness to a critter or to a person, don't be surprised if they learn it.

7. If you're riding ahead of the herd, take a look back every now and then to make sure it's still there.

8. The quickest way to double your money is to fold it over and put it back in your pocket.

9. If you get to thinking you're a person of influence, try ordering somebody else's dog around.

10. And never, ever, miss a good opportunity to shut up.

Wise old bird

A Shropshire farmer went out one day and bought a handsome new stud cockerel for his hens. The farmer put the new cockerel straight into the hen run so he could get on with the job. The young cockerel strode over to the old cockerel and said, 'OK, old chap, it's time you took your retirement.'

The wizened old cockerel said, 'Bah! You can't service all these hens. Look what it's done to me!'

The young cockerel replied, 'Look, face facts. It's time for the old to step down and for the young to step in, so on yer roost, old man.'

The old cockerel said beguilingly, 'Come on, don't be a spoil sport... just let me keep those two old hens over in the far corner. That won't be any skin off your nose.'

But the brash young cockerel wasn't having any of it. 'Push off!' he shouted. 'Your time is over! You're past it! I'm in charge now!'

So the old cockerel thought for a moment and then said to the young pretender, 'Tell you what, young chap: I'll race you round the farmyard. Whoever wins the race gets total dominion over the hen run. And as you think I'm so weak and feeble, why not give me a little bit of a head start?'

The young cockerel said, 'Alright, why not? I'll win anyway.'

So they lined up in one corner of the farmyard, got one of the hens to put them under starter's orders and the old cockerel set off at top speed. About 15 seconds later, the young cockerel set off after him.

They raced round the yard and by the time they reached the front of the farmhouse, the young cockerel was only a few feet behind the old cockerel – and gaining fast. The farmer stood in amazement by the front door of the farmhouse, watching the race, then grabbed his shotgun and... Bang! He shot the young cockerel dead.

He shook his head sadly as he turned to his wife and said, 'Well I'll be blowed, Meg, that's the third gay cockerel I've got lumbered with this month!'

Moral: never under-estimate your elders.

One track mind

A blacksmith with a gambling addiction was in bed with his wife, reading his copy of *Racing Post*. His concentration was distracted by the sniffles of their new baby, who had a slight cold. She was in her cot by the bed.

'Baby's nose is running again,' he murmured, returning to his paper.

His wife snorted. 'That's all you ever think about – racing!'

Rat hunters

An 80-year-old farm labourer from Lancashire went to the doctor for a check-up and the doctor was amazed at how fit he was.

The doctor asked, 'To what do you attribute your good health?'

The old man said, 'I'm a rat hunter and that's why I'm so fit. I'm up well before dawn and I'm out chasing rats up and down the farmyard.'

The doctor said, 'Well, I'm sure that helps, but there's got to be more to it. How old was your dad when he died?'

The old man fired back, 'Who said my dad's dead?'

The doctor said, 'You mean you're 80 years old and your dad's still alive? How old is he?'

The man said, 'He's 100 years old and, in fact, he hunted rats with me this morning, and that's why he's still alive... he's a rat hunter.'

The doctor said, 'Well, that's great, but I'm sure there's more to it. How about your dad's dad? How old was he when he died?'

The old man said, 'Who said my grandpa's dead?'

The doctor said, 'You mean you're 80 years old and your grandfather's still living! How old is he?'

The old timer said, 'He's 118 years old.'

The doctor was becoming sceptical by now and said, 'And don't tell me! He went rat hunting with you this morning too?'

The old man said, 'Oh no! Grandpa couldn't go this morning because he got married.'

The doctor said in amazement, 'Got married! Why would a 118-year-old man want to get married?'

The old man said, 'Who said he wanted to?'

Equestrian thespian

A naive but wealthy racing enthusiast was thrilled when he heard that Arctic Hero, a big winner over the sticks that season, had come up for sale. 'I've always wanted to own a racehorse,' he said to the owner, 'but why do you want to sell him when he's doing so well?'

'Oh,' said the horse's owner, 'I'm fed up with him. He's so vain, and such an actor! Last time out he was winning by several lengths and, would you believe, he slowed down to a canter at the end just so he'd be on camera for a photo finish! And he even made sure his head was turned just the right way so the camera would get his best profile!'

'I don't care if he's Hugh Grant,' said the racing enthusiast, 'I'll take him.'

They went up to Arctic Hero's box and the owner put on his headcollar, ready to lead him out into the yard. 'Okay, Hero,' the owner said loudly. 'Now show this nice man your best impression of a lame horse.'

Point-to-pointing at the porcelain

The village school had arranged a treat for its younger pupils in the 2nd, 3rd and 4th years – a trip to a local point-to-point race meeting. The children were accompanied by two female teachers. After enjoying their picnic, the teachers reckoned that the children should visit the portable toilets before the races began. It was decided that the girls would go with one teacher, and the boys with the other.

The teacher assigned to the boys thought it better to remain outside while they did their business. However after a couple of minutes one of the 3rd year boys came out and told her that none of them could reach the urinals.

Deciding that her duty to the pupils should over-ride modesty, the teacher went into the gents' toilet area and began lifting each boy up, her arms hoisting them under their armpits. She worked her way down the line, including one particular boy whom, she couldn't help but notice, was, shall we say, very mature for his age.

'You must be in the 4th,' she murmured to him, trying hard not to stare.

'No, I'm in the 6th, riding Henry the Hobbit, actually,' he replied. 'But thanks for the lift.'

Did you see that?

Two men were out stalking deer in Scotland. The first man said, 'Did you see that?'

'No,' the second man replied.

'Well, an eagle just flew overhead,' the first man said.

A couple of minutes later, the first man said, 'Did you see that?'

'See what?' the second man asked.

'Are you blind? There was a big wild goat on that hilltop, over there.'

'Oh.'

A few minutes later the first man cried, 'Did you see that?'

By now, the second man was getting annoyed so decided to answer, 'Yes, I did!'

And the first man retorted, 'Then why did you step in it?'

Thank you for not smoking

An extremely rich foreign racing stable owner was known to have a particular dislike of cigarette smoking. One day he was in the UK, touring his magnificent yard near Newmarket and caught one of the lads smoking in the tackroom. Immediately the owner pointed out that the penalty for smoking was instant dismissal, and asked the lad how much he earned. The lad quickly replied, '£100 a week.'

The owner fished £400 in cash out of his pocket, thrust it into the lad's hand and said, 'Right, there's a month's wages, you're sacked.' The lad took the money and left. It was only much later that the owner discovered the young lad was a delivery boy who worked for their saddlery supplier, and had been waiting in the tackroom while the yard manager wrote out a cheque for four new saddles.

It happened in Oakham

A huntsman rode into a village and stopped at the pub for a drink. Unfortunately, the locals had a habit of picking on strangers in the bar. Sure enough, when he finished his drink, he found his horse had been stolen.

He went back into the pub, cracked his whip across the bar and gave a loud blast on his hunting horn.

'Which one of you scumbags stole my horse?!?!?' he demanded with surprising forcefulness.

No one answered.

'Alright, I'm going to have another whisky, and if my

horse isn't back outside by the time I finish, I'm going to do what I did in Oakham! And I don't like to have to do what I did in Oakham!'

Some of the locals shifted restlessly. The man, true to his word, had another whisky, walked outside, and his horse had been returned to the rails.

He mounted up, blew his horn, and started to ride out of the village. The publican wandered out of the bar and asked, 'Excuse me, before you go... what happened in Oakham?'

The huntsman turned in his saddle and said, 'I had to walk home.'

Mancunian cowboy

More than anything, a young lad from Manchester wanted to be a cowboy. He finally saved up enough money to get to the US and eventually found a rancher who took pity on him and gave the lad a chance.

'This,' said the rancher, showing him a rope, 'is a lasso. We use it to catch cows.'

'I see,' said the young man, trying to seem knowledgeable as he examined the lasso. 'And what do you use for bait?'

Too smart for his own good

A shepherd was watching his flock in a field intersected by a lonely road. Suddenly a brand new Porsche Cayenne screeched to a halt next to him. The driver, a young man dressed in a Paul Smith suit, Gucci shoes, Alexander McQueen sunglasses and a Fendi tie, rolled the window down and asked the shepherd: 'If I guess how many sheep you have out there, will you give one of them to me?'

The shepherd looked at the young man, then at the sheep grazing beyond and said, 'Alright.'

The young man parked the Porsche Cayenne, dialled up a number on his Blackberry, entered a NASA site, scanned the ground using his SatNav device, opened a database and 60 Excel tables filled with algorithms, then printed a 150-page report on his high-tech mini-printer. He turned to the shepherd and announced, 'You have exactly 103 animals here.'

The shepherd answered, 'That's correct. You may have your sheep.'

The young man opened the tailgate of his Porsche Cayenne and put the animal inside.

He was just about to drive off when the shepherd stopped him: 'If I guess your profession, will you let me have my sheep back?'

The townie was confident: 'Yes, why not?'

The shepherd said firmly, 'You are a management consultant.'

'How did you know?' asked the young man, amazed.

'It's obvious,' answered the shepherd. 'First, you come here without being invited. Second, you charge me a sheep to tell me something I already know. Third, you do not understand anything about what I do, because you took my Border Collie.'

Mistaken identity

On a cold, dawn hillside in Cumbria a ewe was heavily in labour but nothing was happening. The farmer, fearing a complicated delivery, rang the vets' emergency number on his mobile phone only to find it was answered by a locum vet he had never spoken to before. 'This ewe is lambing and I think something's going wrong,' shouted the farmer down the phone.

'Is this her first lamb?' asked the vet.

'No, you idiot!' screamed the reply. 'This is the farmer!'

A fun day out

A sheep breeder was taking a lorry load of prize ewes to a local show in Surrey. Just a few miles from the showground his lorry broke down, so he hailed a passing cattle truck which, fortunately, was empty, and said to the driver he'd give him £100 if he'd take the sheep to the show.

The lorry driver agreed, so he loaded them up and went off, while the breeder started the long wait for the breakdown services to turn up. About an hour later he was amazed to see the cattle truck come back and stop beside him, the sheep all still loaded up in the back.

He shouted 'But I gave you £100 to take them all to the show!'

The driver replied agreeably, 'Oh, but the tickets only came to £50. So I'll take them to the cinema now.'

Bully for you

An old bull and a young bull were quietly grazing at the top of a hill, overlooking a herd of heifers. After a while, the young bull turned to the old one and said, 'Hey, why don't we charge down and have us a couple of those heifers?'

The old bull gazed calmly over at him and replied, 'No, let's walk down slowly and have 'em all.'

Local knowledge

A Derbyshire sheep farmer and his wife were driving around Carmarthenshire, looking for good collie pups to bring back to raise, train and sell on. They arrived at a small town with a typically Welsh name, consisting of numerous consonants and few vowels. They began to argue over how it should be pronounced, but couldn't agree. Eventually, they decided to stop for a cup of tea. As the waitress brought their orders to the table, the sheep farmer said to her, 'My wife and I can't agree how to pronounce the name of this place. Could you please tell us how it should be pronounced?'

The waitress put her tray down and said very slowly, 'M..c..D..o..n..a..l..d..s'

Lighten up

A farmer and his wife were driving back from a livestock auction late one night, when a police car pulled them over to the side of the road. The police officer approached the driver, who rolled down his window.

'Are you aware that you're driving without rear lights, sir?' asked the officer.

With that, the farmer flung open his door and ran around to the rear of the car, groaning and clutching his forehead. He was so upset that the officer took pity on him, and said kindly, 'It's not exactly a hanging offence, sir. In fact it really isn't serious.'

'Of course it's serious!' cried the man. 'I've lost the trailer with my sheep inside it!'

Made in Britain

A three-year-old girl had just been with her mother to see the neighbour's new-born lamb. They went into the house and the little girl ran to find her daddy so she could tell him all about it.

'Tell me,' asked her father, 'is it a boy lamb or a girl lamb?'

'A girl,' replied the little girl.

'And how could you tell? Did your Mum ask Mrs Jenkins?' asked the father.

'No,' replied the little girl. 'Mum looked between the lamb's back legs. I think it must be printed on its tummy.'

Hounds of hell

Up in Heaven, St Peter, St Paul and St John were standing in the back yard, bored. 'Tell you what,' said St Peter. 'Let's put on a dog show. That will give us something interesting to do.'

'Small problem, though,' said St Paul. 'We've already got all the best dogs here in Heaven. There's no competition.'

'Ah, I have an idea,' said St John. 'Let's invite the Devil to compete. He only has ugly, scrawny, bad-tempered dogs, so we're bound to win every class.'

The Devil jumped at their idea. 'We would be delighted to compete,' he said, 'and our dogs are bound to win every class.'

'Don't be silly,' said St Peter. 'We have all the finest dogs here. How could you possibly beat us?'

'Simple,' answered the Devil. 'We've got all the judges.'

Bad taste

The local Young Farmers' Club had arranged an annual dinner for its committee, but the catering was terrible. One committee member complained to the Club Secretary.

'The food was awful,' he said. 'Can you do something about it?'

'Not at this point,' replied the Secretary. 'You'll just have to bring it up at the next committee meeting.'

What a drag

Two deer stalkers were dragging their dead deer across the moor back to their truck. Another stalker joined them, pulling his along too.

'I say,' he said, 'I don't want to teach grandmothers to suck eggs, but you'll find it much easier if you drag the deer the other way round. Then the antlers won't dig into the ground.'

And with that, he set off ahead of them. The first two stalkers decided to try it. A little while later one said to the other, 'You know, that chap was right. This is a lot easier!'

'Yes,' the other added, 'but we're getting further away from the truck.'

Racing favourite

Worried about her husband, a woman went to see a psychiatrist. 'He thinks he's a race horse,' she said. 'He sleeps standing up, whinnies instead of speaking, and even insists on eating pony nuts for breakfast. It's terrible.'

'How long has this been going on?' asked the psychiatrist.

'Several months now,' replied the woman.

The psychiatrist thought carefully. 'You've let this go too far. Your husband will require lengthy counselling and psycho-analysis, which is not available on the NHS. This could be very expensive.'

'Money doesn't matter, I don't care about the expense,'

said the woman. 'I'm prepared to pay whatever it costs to stop my husband thinking he's a horse.'

'I must warn you it could be thousands of pounds,' said the psychiatrist. 'Can you really afford all that money?'

'Oh yes,' said the woman. 'He's already won the Cheltenham Gold Cup and the Epsom Derby and now he's got full sponsorship from Pol Roger.'

Rear guard action

Two men went red deer stalking in the Cairngorms every year without success. Finally they came up with a foolproof plan. They got themselves a very authentic-looking hind costume and learned the mating call of the female. The plan was to hide in the costume, lure in the stag, then leap out of the costume and shoot him.

So, they set themselves up on the edge of a clearing, in their costume, and began to give the red deer love call. Before long their call was answered by a stag in the forest.

They called again and the stag answered, closer to them. They called again, the stag answered, and came crashing out of the forest and into the clearing. As the male's pounding hoof-beats sounded ever closer, the man in the front of the costume said, 'OK, let's get out and get him.'

After a moment that seemed like an eternity, the man in the back half shouted 'The zip's stuck! What are we going to do?'

'Well,' said the man in the front half, 'I'm going to start nibbling grass. And you'd better brace yourself.'

How to identify a farrier

He watches the way people walk and thinks to himself, 'With the right shoes I could compensate for that.'

He thinks it's normal to come home to messages on the answering machine from women he doesn't know, saying they need him desperately.

He can spend 12 hours a day bent over, but his back aches after standing upright for ten minutes.

If someone is hammering nails on a building site, he will stop and listen carefully.

He's not a lap dancer, but his customers still spend more time looking at his backside than at his face.

He thinks working from 8am to 8pm is a half day.

He looks ten years younger but feels ten years older than his real age.

Bang to rights

An 80-year-old farmer went to his doctor for his annual check-up. The doctor asked him how was feeling. The 80-year-old said, 'I've never felt better. I have a 20-year-old bride who is pregnant with my child. What do you think about that?'

The doctor considered his question for a minute and said, 'I have a friend who is an avid member of a shoot and he never misses a season. One day when he was out shooting, a pheasant suddenly flew up. In his hurry, my friend accidentally picked up his umbrella rather than his gun. He raised it, aimed at the pheasant and shouted, 'Bang, bang!' The pheasant dropped out of the sky. What do you think about that?'

The 80-year-old farmer said, 'I'd say somebody else shot that pheasant.'

The doctor replied, 'My point exactly.'

A moose in the hoose

A Scotsman was visiting a friend in Canada. Both enjoyed shooting.

They went hunting for deer, when all of a sudden, a moose popped up in front of them. It was so unexpected, neither of them had a chance to fire.

The Scotsman was shaken. 'Hoot mon, wit was tha'?'

'That was a moose', the Canadian replied.

'A moose? Good Lord, I'd hate to see the size of yer rats!'

Tale with a twist

A farmer's wife went to the doctor with a badly-sprained ankle. The doctor advised her not to put weight on it for two weeks.

'Will I be able to drive a tractor when it's better?' she asked.

'Most certainly,' replied the doctor.

'That's good,' said the woman. 'Because I've never driven a tractor before in my life.'

Paws for thought

Some years ago the Government decided to crack down on dog owners who had not purchased licences for their pets. Police were given instructions to stop dog owners at random and check their licences or warn them to go and buy one.

One elderly farmer who was driving his tractor down the lane was stopped by a policeman. He asked what the problem was. The officer pointed to a large sheepdog sitting in the tractor cab and said, 'Does your dog have a licence?'

'Oh, no,' replied the old farmer. 'He doesn't need one, because I always drive.'

Step in the right direction

A farm manager agreed to take on a work-experience pupil and he decided to teach her a few things about how to handle the animals.

'I want you to imagine you had walked into that field and realised the gate had been left open. Suddenly, you see 20 bullocks galloping straight at you. You have only seconds to take action. What steps would you take?'

The girl thought for a moment. 'Very long and fast ones, Mr Jenkins.'

The wisdom of youth

A child was taken to the Secretary's tent at the CLA gamefair. It appeared he had lost his mother.

The Secretary smiled kindly at the little boy and said, 'I'm sure we'll find your Mummy soon. What's she like?'

The little boy thought for a moment. 'Whippers-In and Hunt Secretaries,' he said firmly.

Puddle trouble

A man driving down a country road was forced to stop before a giant puddle which covered the entire road. Looking to one side, the man noticed a farmer leaning on a fence.

'Do you think it's safe to cross?' the man asked.

'I reckon so,' replied the farmer.

The puddle immediately swallowed the car as the man drove in. It was so deep that he had to roll his window down to swim out. As his head broke the surface, the man said to the farmer, 'I thought you said I could safely drive through this puddle!'

'Well, I thought so!' said the farmer, scratching his head. 'It only come up chest-high on my ducks!'

Grin and bear it

A farmer had a smash up on his quad bike and dislocated his shoulder. He was taken to the Accident and Emergency unit at the nearest hospital, where the medics attempted to put his shoulder back into place without an anaesthetic. The farmer shouted and yelled in agony.

'Pull yourself together!' said a junior doctor. 'There's a woman about to have a baby in the next cubicle and she's not making half the noise you are.'

'Maybe not,' screamed the farmer. 'But they're not trying to put it back!'

Fuss on a bus

The bus was crowded with people on their way into town for market day. At a secluded stop on a country lane, an old man struggled on to the bus. No-one gave him a seat.

As the bus shook and rattled along the lanes, the old man's walking stick slipped on the floor of the bus, and he fell down.

The old man got up with some difficulty and composed himself. A young yokel sitting nearby turned to him and said, 'You know, if you put a little rubber thingy on the end of your stick, it won't slip.'

The old man snapped back, 'Well, if your dad had done the same thing sixteen years ago, I'd have a seat on this bus.'

Get well soonish

A bossy lady on the village fete committee was taken ill and had to spend two weeks in hospital. While there, she received a Get Well card from the rest of the committee. Under their signatures, someone had written 'The decision to send this card was carried by seven votes to six.'

Mooooody

A farmer's wife was having a physical examination for her health insurance and was extremely embarrassed because she was so overweight. As she took off her final item of clothing, she blushed. 'I'm so ashamed, doctor,' she said, 'I really have let myself go.'

The doctor was busy examining her ears. 'Don't worry, my dear. You don't look that awful.'

'Really, doctor?' she asked, perking up.

The doctor brandished a tongue depressor close to her face and said, 'No, of course not. Now, would you open your mouth please, and say moo.'

Can't get the staff

The licensee of the *Old White Horse* was furious when one of his young barmaids arrived late yet again. 'Angela,' he yelled, 'you should have been here at opening time!'

'Why?' asked the barmaid. 'What happened?'

Small pleasures

A man went into a farm supply shop and bought a pair of walking boots two sizes too small for him. When the assistant asked him why, he said 'My wife has left me, my gardening business has gone bankrupt, and my dog died last week. Now the only pleasure I have left in life is when I take my boots off at the end of the day.'

No cause for alarm

Four farm hands were always playing cards in the hay barn when the farm manager wasn't around. One day he spotted them at it, so he thought he would give them a fright to teach them a lesson. He rang the fire alarm bell three times, then waited to watch their reaction. To his amazement, nothing happened. Then, a couple of minutes later, the barman from the pub across the road crossed the farmyard with four pints of beer.

Talking lawn mowers

A country squire was sitting quietly reading the newspaper when his wife sneaked up behind him and whacked him on the head with a rolling pin.

'What was that for?' he asked.

'That was for the piece of paper in your trouser pocket with the name Tilly written on it,' she snapped.

'Don't be silly,' he said, smiling. 'Last week, when I went to the auctions, that was the brand name of a ride-on lawn mower I wanted to bid for.'

She looked satisfied, apologised, and went off to cook supper. Three days later, he was sitting in his chair once more, reading the paper, when she whacked him on the head with the rolling pin, knocking him out. When he came round, he said, 'What the hell was that for?'

'That ride-on lawn mower rang up and asked to speak to you.'

Army days

A retired Army General ran into his former old batman, also retired, in a village pub and spent the rest of the evening trying to persuade him to come back to work for him as his valet.

'Your duties will be exactly the same as they were in the Army,' the General assured him. 'It'll all come back to you very quickly.'

The next morning at eight o'clock sharp, the ex-batman entered the ex-General's bedroom, pulled open the curtains, gave the General a gentle shake, walked round to the other side of the bed, slapped the General's wife on her bottom and said, 'Right me love, it's time for you to run along back to the village.'

No maids a-milking

In the small hours of the morning, an elderly dairy farmer was rushed to hospital having suffered a heart-attack. At one point the medical staff thought he might die, so summoned everyone to the bedside. The farmer's eyelids flickered as he asked who was there, and all his family and all his farm labourers called out to say: yes, they were there. At that, the farmer sat bolt upright in bed and shouted, 'You're ALL here? Then who the hell is milking the cows this morning?'

Wheel strength

A strong, broad-shouldered young farm-hand was boasting that he could out-do anyone in a feat of strength. He especially made fun of one of the older farm-hands.

Eventually, the old farm-hand had had enough. 'Why don't you put your money where your mouth is,' he said. 'I will bet a week's wages that I can carry something in a wheelbarrow over to that barn that you won't be able to wheel back.'

'You're on, old man,' the braggart replied. 'Let's see what you got.'

The old man reached out and grabbed the wheelbarrow by the handles. Then, nodding to the young man, he said, 'All right, get in.'

Prize effort

Bert stopped by his friend Frank's farm one evening to say hello. He noticed that Frank's car was parked there and the animals were all settled in for the night. But Frank was nowhere to be found. Eventually, Bert decided to have a look in the field, in case there had been an accident. To Bert's amazement there was Frank, out in the middle of it, just standing there.

'What on earth are you doing?' shouted Bert to his friend.

'Trying to win a Nobel Prize,' Frank shouted back.

'How are you going to do that?' asked Bert, in astonishment.

'Well,' announced Frank, 'I've heard they give the Nobel Prize to people who are out standing in their field.'

Welcome with a wag

A woman wrote to a country house hotel on the Isle of Wight prior to booking her holiday there, asking if they would allow her to bring her Cairn terrier.

A few days later she received a letter from the hotel which said...

'Dear Madam,

This hotel has been established since 1902. Not once in its history have its proprietors been obliged to ring the police to eject a disorderly dog from the bar, to request repeatedly that a dog should turn down the noise from the television, to deal with a dog's endless complaints about the quality of food and service, or to suffer a bounced cheque written by a dog. Similarly, no dog has ever been found to have set the bedclothes on fire from having fallen asleep with a lit cigarette, nor has a dog ever been responsible for stealing towels, bathrobes, ashtrays, the Gideon's Bible or the telephone directory from a room. We conclude, therefore, by informing you that your dog will be most welcome at our hotel. And if the dog can vouch for its owner, you, too, will be most welcome.'

Off track

A landowner known as a 'bit of a character' was approached by the railway authorities who were planning a new rail track through one of his fields. They offered him a huge sum of money in compensation for the land, many times its real value, but he turned it down.

'Why on earth did you do that?' asked a friend. 'That field's nothing but thistles; it's been set-aside for years, and the money would keep you in malt whisky for the rest of your life.'

'That's true enough,' said the landowner. 'But I can't be bothered to go out there and open the ruddy gate every time a train's coming through.'

Hair today...

An old man was sitting on a bench by the village green, staring at a young man.

The young man walked up to the bench and sat down. He had spiked hair in all different colours: green, red, orange, blue, yellow. The old man just stared.

The young man said sarcastically, 'What's the matter? Never done anything wild in your life?'

Without batting an eye, the old man replied, 'I got drunk once and had sex with a parrot. I was just wondering if you were my son.'

Firefighting

A fire broke out in a cornfield on a farm in Somerset. The County fire department was called, but despite all their high-tech equipment the blaze proved to be more than they could handle and they withdrew. Someone suggested that the village volunteer fire crew be called. Though there was doubt that they could be of much help, the call was made anyway.

Ten minutes later, the village fire crew arrived in a dilapidated old fire engine. Without hesitation they drove straight at the fire and screeched to a halt in the middle of the flames. The village firemen jumped off the vehicle into the blaze and frantically started spraying water in all directions. Soon, they had snuffed out the fire. The farmer was impressed with the village fire crew's work and was extremely grateful that his farm had been spared. The next day he presented them with a cheque for £1,000. A local news reporter asked them what they planned to do with the money.

'Well,' the village chief fire officer replied, 'The first thing we're going to do is get the brakes fixed on that old fire engine.'

In other words...

A young farm labourer at a very large farm got his courage together and went to see the manager to ask for a pay rise. When he entered the office, the farm's accountant was there too. 'I'm due a pay rise,' stammered the young lad.

'Well, young man,' said the accountant while the farm manager nodded wisely, 'Due to the fluctuational predisposition of the global competitive farming economic climate, along with current and upcoming EC legislation, juxtaposed against the individual staff productivity within this particular sphere of enterprise, in my judgement I feel it would be fiscally inappropriate to elevate exponentially your specific increment.'

'Do what?' said the puzzled lad. 'I don't get it.'

'Exactly,' said the farm manager.

Responsible girl

A seed merchant telephoned the manager of another, similar local business and shouted angrily, 'In your reference for Miss Jones, you claimed she was a responsible worker!'

'She is,' came the reply. 'In the time she was here, the oats got mixed in with the barley, the main silo burnt down, the computer system crashed on seventeen occasions, fourteen customers were told precisely where they could stick their orders and took their business elsewhere, and I nearly had a nervous breakdown. And in each case, she was responsible.'

Good deal

'Last week I got a lovely pot-bellied pig for my husband.'
'I know your husband. That sounds like a fair swap.'

Over-staffed

A loyal old game-keeper had worked for a rather stingy country squire for 40 years before he finally plucked up courage to ask for a pay rise. When he did, the squire said, 'Sam, the stock market's down and my investments are doing badly right now. I can't afford it.' The poor chap was crest-fallen and said 'But I'm doing the work of three gamekeepers!' The squire was furious and roared, 'Three gamekeepers! Tell me their names, and I'll sack them!'

Best practice

A townie was completely lost in Cumbria and stopped at the next village he drove to. 'What's the quickest way to Upper Waddingford?' he asked a local.

The local scratched his head.

'Are you walking or driving?' he asked the stranger.

'I'm driving.'

'That's the quickest way!'

Transport trouble

A pig breeder decided that he could finally afford a lorry after years of making do with a trailer. He went to see a suitable vehicle and asked to go out for a test drive in it. After they'd been round the lanes the dealer looked over at him and said, 'I think you could honestly say that this lorry is the opportunity of a lifetime.' And the pig breeder said, 'Yes, I can hear it knocking.' Taking this as an insult, the dealer said indignantly, 'We stand behind every lorry we sell.' So the pig breeder said, 'Yes, but are you prepared to push them?'

Audience awareness

A famous flower arranger was asked to give a speech at a local WI guest luncheon. She asked the chairwoman to give her some details about the audience. 'You know the kind of thing,' she said, 'Numbers, broken down by age and sex.' And the Chairwoman replied, 'Yes, I'm afraid they are.'

Vegetable garden

Two elderly ladies met at the village shop, after not seeing one another for some time.

After inquiring about each other's health, one asked how the other's husband was doing.

'Oh! Albert died last week. He went out to the garden to dig up a cabbage for dinner, had a heart attack and dropped down dead, right there in the middle of the vegetable patch!'

'Oh dear! I'm very sorry,' replied her friend 'What did you do?'

'Opened a can of beans instead.'

Rough translation

A little girl at the village school was sent to the headteacher for swearing in class.

'We really can't tolerate language like that, Jenny,' said the Head. 'Wherever did you hear it?'

'Mummy says it,' replied the girl.

'Surely not,' said the Head. 'And I hope you don't even know what it means.'

'Yes I do,' piped up the little girl. 'It means "a cow is standing on my foot".'

Blending in

An elderly female zebra had delighted visitors at the zoo for many years, so when she was due for retirement, the zoo keeper arranged for her to go to the countryside, to his friend's 'open farm' where she could be spoiled and pampered throughout her last days.

The zebra had never seen domestic animals before, so when she arrived at the open farm she decided to find out what all these interesting new species were and what they did. The first creature she approached was small and furry with long ears.

'What are you, and what do you do?' asked the zebra.

'I'm a rabbit,' replied the creature, 'and children love to cuddle me.'

Next she approached a larger creature with curved horns.

'What are you, and what do you do?' she asked.

'I'm a goat, and the children like to feed me,' answered

the goat.

Then, the zebra spotted a much larger creature in the adjacent paddock. It was very like her, about the same size, but with a fuzzy grey coat and long ears.

'My goodness, what are you, and what do you do?' asked the zebra.

'I'm a donkey, and I just stroll calmly around the paddock so everyone can admire me,' replied the donkey.

'Well as you're an equid, we're related,' said the zebra. 'May I come and live with you in your paddock?'

But the donkey looked down her nose at the zebra.

'Well, I suppose so,' she said reluctantly, 'but you'd have to change out of those AWFUL pyjamas first.'

Farm diversification

A husband and wife were driving down a rural lane on their way to a country house hotel, where they had booked a weekend break. They came to a pool of muddy water in the road and as they attempted to drive through, the car became bogged down and finally stalled. After a few minutes of trying to get the car out by themselves, they were relieved to see a young farmer coming down the lane, driving a tractor.

He stopped when he saw the couple in trouble and offered to tow the car out of the mud for £50. The husband accepted and minutes later the car was free. The farmer said to the husband,

'You know, yours is the tenth car I've towed out of that mud today.'

The husband looked around at the fields incredulously and asked the farmer,

'When do you have time to plough your land then? At night?'

'No,' the young farmer replied seriously, 'Night is when I pump the water into the road.'

Journey to nowhere

Two townies were partying and drinking beer in the woods when all of a sudden there was a heavy thunderstorm. The two ran for about 10 minutes in the pouring rain, finally reaching their car just as the rain let up. They jumped in the car, started it up and headed down the road, laughing and, of course, still drinking one beer after the other.

All of a sudden an old man's face appeared at the passenger door and tapped lightly on the window. 'Look at the window,' screamed the passenger. 'There's an old man's face! Is it a ghost?'

The old man kept knocking, so the driver, struggling to keep the car on the road, said, 'Open the window a little and ask him what he wants.' The passenger rolled his window down part way and, scared out of his wits, asked 'What do you want?'

The old man softly replied, 'You have any tobacco?'

The passenger, terrified, looked at the driver and said, 'He wants tobacco!' 'Well, offer him a cigarette! HURRY!!' the driver replied.

The passenger fumbled around with the pack and handed the old man a cigarette through the window, then yelled to the driver, 'Step on it!!!'

Now doing about 80 miles an hour, they regained their confidence and started laughing again. 'What did you think of that?' the passenger asked.

'I don't know what's going on,' said the driver. 'How could that doddery old bloke keep up with us?'

All of a sudden, there was another knock on the window and the old man was staring in at them once more.

'Aaaaaaaaaaaaaa! There he is again!' the passenger yelled, as they sped along.

'Well, see what he wants now!' shouted the driver.

The passenger rolled down the window a little way and stammered, 'Yes?'

'Do you have a light?' the old man quietly asked. The passenger threw a lighter out at him, rolled up the window and again yelled, 'STEP ON IT!'

They were now doing about 100 miles an hour, trying to forget what they had just witnessed. Suddenly, there was more knocking again.

'HE'S BACK!' The passenger rolled down the window and shrieked, 'WHAT DO YOU WANT?'

The old man gently replied, 'Do you want some help getting out of the mud?'

Hidden danger

Some tourists were driving through the sleepy Devonshire countryside, and decided to stop at the village post office to buy some postcards. As they entered the premises, they noticed a large sign saying 'Beware of the dog.'

Looking around, all they could see was an elderly terrier

curled up asleep by the counter.

'Is that the dog that's meant to be dangerous?' asked one of the tourists.

'Yes,' replied the post-mistress.' The old terrier woke up briefly, looked at the tourists, wagged his stumpy little tail a few times, then went back to sleep.

'He doesn't look dangerous at all. In fact I'd say he's rather a sweet old chap,' said the second tourist. 'Why have you put that sign up saying 'Beware of the dog?''

'Well,' replied the post-mistress, 'Before I put that sign up, everyone kept tripping over him.'

Tricky chicken

A man was driving along a country lane when he remembered he had to make a phone call. He had forgotten to bring his mobile phone and was miles from a pay phone, so he decided to stop at the next farmhouse he found.

As he was approaching a house, he noticed a three-legged chicken racing along the road. He followed the chicken and clocked it at 45 miles per hour.

When the man got to the farmhouse he asked the farmer about the chicken. The farmer replied, 'Well, when I was at university I studied genetics. Round here we love chicken and we're all specially fond of the drumsticks, so I thought I'd see if I could breed a three-legged chicken. I did, and that's what you saw.'

The man was highly impressed.

'Does it taste good?' he asked.

'Don't know. Never been able to catch one yet.'

Coyote control
(supposedly true – original source unknown)

We think we have trouble controlling the badger population at the moment in our countryside. A few years ago, the Sierra Club and the U.S. Forest Service were presenting an alternative to the Wyoming ranchers for controlling the coyote population.

It seems that after years of the ranchers using the tried

and trusted methods of shooting and/or trapping the coyotes, the 'tree-huggers' had a come up with a 'more humane' solution.

What they proposed was for the coyotes to be captured alive, the males castrated and let loose again and thus the population would be controlled. This programme was proposed to the Wyoming Wool and Sheep Grower's Association by the Sierra Club and the USFS.

All of the local ranchers paused to consider this controversial idea for a couple of minutes.

Finally, an old boy in the back stood up, tipped his hat back and said, 'Son, I don't think you understand the problem. Those coyotes ain't makin' love to our sheep – they're eatin' 'em!'

Let the buyer beware

A dog breeder from America was driving by a farm in Yorkshire when he spotted a superb, apparently pure-bred Saluki. He stopped, found the farmer, and said, 'Your dog looks really good. I'll give you a thousand pounds for him.'

'Nay, he doesn't look so good, and besides he's not for sale,' grunted the farmer in reply.

'Well I think he looks incredibly good, so I'll give you two thousand pounds for him.' said the man.

'I tell thee, yon dog doesn't look so good,' replied the farmer, 'but if you want him that badly, then aye, you can have him.'

The man put the Saluki into the back of his car and took it home. The next morning he was on the phone to the farmer, shouting with fury. 'You old so-and-so,' he ranted, 'That dog you sold me is blind! You swindled me!'

'Nay, I never did,' replied the farmer. 'I told you he didn't look so good.'

Vegetable nostalgia

Three old ladies were sitting side by side in their retirement home, reminiscing. The first lady recalled shopping at the village green-grocers and indicated with her hands, the length and thickness of a cucumber she could buy for a penny.

The second old lady nodded knowingly, adding that onions used to be much bigger and cheaper too, and demonstrated the size of two big onions she could buy for a penny each.

The third old lady remarked, 'I can't hear a word you're saying, but I well remember the fellow you're talking about.'

Who's a clever boy then?

Did you hear about the gamekeeper who crossed a carrier pigeon with a woodpecker?

He got a bird that not only delivers messages to their destination, but knocks on the door when it gets there.

Ask a silly question...

A Shropshire farmer and his wife had taken themselves off on a motoring holiday in the United States. One day they were driving around some lonely rural roads in West Virginia, when they happened upon a large pile of stones in the middle of the road. A red light was perched on top of the pile.

They pulled up, wondering what to do next, when a local man pulled up beside them on his motorbike. The farmer's wife wound down her window and asked what the red light was for.

'It's to stop drivers hittin' the pile of stones, ma'am,' said the motorbiker.

'But what is the pile of stones for?' asked the farmer's wife.

'Well, to put the red light on, of course,' said the local. 'Y'all have a nice day now, ya hear?'

Girl power

Three ramblers were hiking through the woods when they came upon a wide, raging, violent river. Needing to get to the other side, the first man prayed, 'God, please give me the strength to cross this river.' Poof! God gave him big arms and strong legs and he was able to swim across in about two hours, having almost drowned twice.

So, the second man prayed, 'God, please give me strength and the tools to cross the river.' Poof! God gave him a rowing boat and strong arms and strong legs and he was able to row across in about an hour after almost capsizing once.

Seeing what happened to the first two men, the third man prayed, 'God, please give me the strength, the tools and the intelligence to cross the river. Poof! He was turned into a woman. She checked the map, walked one hundred yards up-stream and strode across the bridge.

Love machine

A little town in the valley had one of the highest birth rates in Wales, and this phenomenon attracted the attention of the sociologists at Aberystwyth University.

They applied for a grant; got massive funding; moved to the town; set up their computers; and began designing their questionnaires, etc.

While the students were busy getting ready for their big research project, the head of studies decided to go to visit the little town in person. He went into the local pub, sat down on a barstool, ordered his pint, and while he was drinking it, he told the publican why he was there. Then, he asked the landlord if he had any idea why the birth rate was so high.

'Surely to goodness, I do,' said the owner. 'Every morning the six o'clock train comes through the valley and sounds its horn for the crossing. It wakes everybody up, and, well, it's too late to go back to sleep, and it's too early to get up.'

Chicken pancake

An East Anglian farmer phoned the vet and said, 'Two of my chickens have stopped laying.'

'Really,' asked the vet, 'how do you know?'

'Because,' the farmer replied, 'I just ran over the b*st*rds in my tractor.'

You may also like to read:

The Tippling Philosopher
Jeremy James
A collection of twenty hilarious and true pub-told stories, gathered from the bars and pubs of the Clun Valley.
£12

What a Chap Really Wants in Bed
Giles Catchpole & Roderick Emery
"Highly amusing shooting and fishing tales [accompanied by Copplestone's witty cartoons] – the perfect bed-time read." – *Shooting Times*
£20

The Temptation & Downfall of the Vicar of Stanton Lacy
Peter Klein
"A true story: more real than any historical novel – more moving, more evocative, more human." – John Fowles
£12

Maynard: the Adventures of a Bacon Curer
Maynard Davies
An extraordinary memoir from one of the last apprentice-boy bacon curers, who today is an authority in his field. A compelling life-story.
£9.99

Available from Merlin Unwin Books, 7 Corve Street, Ludlow SY8 1DB.
To order: tel. 01584 877456 or online: www.merlinunwin.co.uk